HAL•LEONARD
INSTRUMENTAL
PLAY-ALONG

AUDIO
ACCESS
INCLUDED

PLAYBACK+
eed • Pitch • Balance • Loop

TENOR SAX

T0088840

Audio arrangements by Peter Deneff

To access audio visit:
www.halleonard.com/mylibrary

Enter Code
6444-5831-6517-0980

ISBN 978-1-70516-357-3

Visit Hal Leonard Online at
www.halleonard.com

Contact us:
Hal Leonard
7777 West Bluemound Road
Milwaukee, WI 53213
Email: info@halleonard.com

In Europe, contact:
Hal Leonard Europe Limited
42 Wigmore Street
Marylebone, London, W1U 2RN
Email: info@halleonardeurope.com

In Australia, contact:
Hal Leonard Australia Pty. Ltd.
4 Lentara Court
Cheltenham, Victoria, 3192 Australia
Email: info@halleonard.com.au

ALL OF YOU

TENOR SAX

Music and Lyrics by
LIN-MANUEL MIRANDA

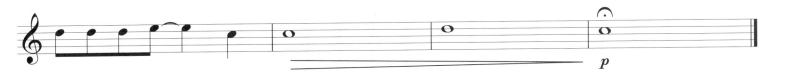

COLOMBIA, MI ENCANTO

TENOR SAX

Music and Lyrics by
LIN-MANUEL MIRANDA

THE FAMILY MADRIGAL

TENOR SAX

Music and Lyrics by
LIN-MANUEL MIRANDA

DOS ORUGUITAS

TENOR SAX

Music and Lyrics by
LIN-MANUEL MIRANDA

SURFACE PRESSURE

TENOR SAX

Music and Lyrics by
LIN-MANUEL MIRANDA

WAITING ON A MIRACLE

TENOR SAX

Music and Lyrics by
LIN-MANUEL MIRANDA

rit.

WE DON'T TALK ABOUT BRUNO

TENOR SAX

Music and Lyrics by
LIN-MANUEL MIRANDA

WHAT ELSE CAN I DO?

TENOR SAX

Music and Lyrics by
LIN-MANUEL MIRANDA

To Coda ⊕

D.S. al Coda

CODA ⊕

THE RAINBOW CONNECTION
from THE MUPPET MOVIE

Words and Music by
PAUL WILLIAMS and KENNETH L. ASCHER

Moderately, with a lilt

THE AVENGERS
from THE AVENGERS

Composed by ALAN SILVESTRI

Moderately, with intensity

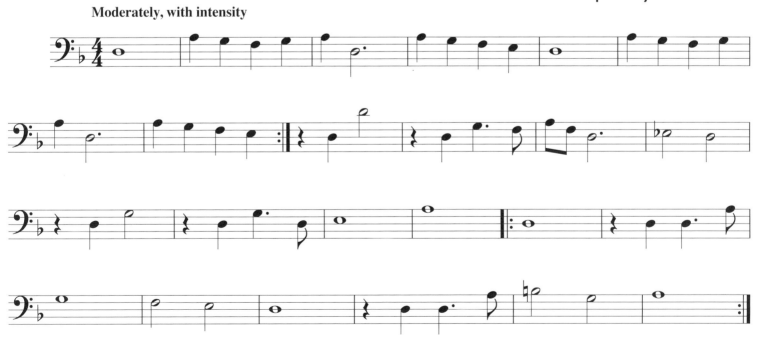

HALLELUJAH

Words and Music by LEONARD COHEN

Copyright © 1985 Sony Music Publishing (US) LLC
This arrangement Copyright © 2023 Sony Music Publishing (US) LLC
All Rights Administered by Sony Music Publishing (US) LLC, 424 Church Street, Suite 1200, Nashville, TN 37219
International Copyright Secured   All Rights Reserved

KERNKRAFT 400

By EMANUEL GUENTHER and FLORIAN SENFTER

Copyright © 1999 UKW Publishing Florian Senfter
This arrangement Copyright © 2023 UKW Publishing Florian Senfter
All Rights Administered in the U.S. by Downtown DLJ Songs o/b/o Budde Music Inc.
All Rights Reserved   Used by Permission

HAPPY

Words and Music by PHARRELL WILLIAMS

Moderately Fast

SKYFALL

from the Motion Picture SKYFALL

Words and Music by
ADELE ADKINS and PAUL EPWORTH

Moderately Slow, Mysterious

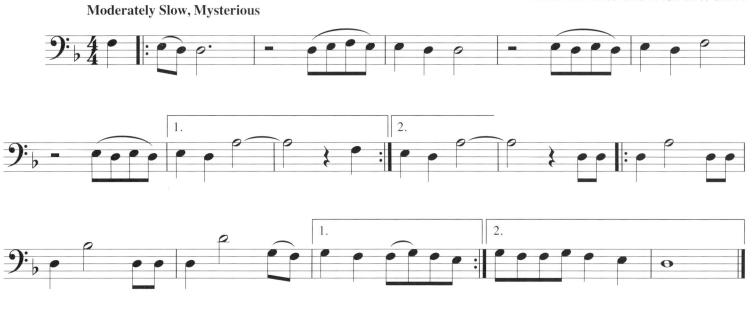

HAVANA

Words and Music by CAMILA CABELLO, LOUIS BELL, PHARRELL WILLIAMS, ADAM FEENEY, ALI TAMPOSI, JEFFERY LAMAR WILLIAMS, BRIAN LEE, ANDREW WOTMAN, BRITTANY HAZZARD and KAAN GUNESBERK

Moderately, with a Latin Groove

HIGH HOPES

Words and Music by BRENDON URIE, WILLIAM LOBBAN BEAN, JONAS JEBERG, SAMUEL HOLLANDER, JACOB SINCLAIR, JENNY OWEN YOUNGS, ILSEY JUBER, LAUREN PRITCHARD and TAYLA PARX

Moderately

Señorita

**Words and Music by CAMILA CABELLO,
CHARLOTTE AITCHISON, JACK PATTERSON,
SHAWN MENDES, MAGNUS HOIBERG,
BENJAMIN LEVIN, ALI TAMPOSI
and ANDREW WOTMAN**

Moderate Latin Groove

SEVEN NATION ARMY

Words and Music by JACK WHITE

Moderate Rock

HEAVEN

Words and Music by SHY CARTER,
LINDSAY RIMES and MATTHEW MCGINN

Slow Rock

DYNAMITE

Words and Music by
JESSICA AGOMBAR and DAVID STEWART

Moderately Fast

COUNTING STARS

Words and Music by RYAN TEDDER

Moderately

SUCKER

Words and Music by NICK JONAS, JOSEPH JONAS,
MILES ALE, MUSTAFA AHMED, RYAN TEDDER, LOUIS BELL,
ADAM FEENEY, KEVIN JONAS and HOMER STEINWEISS

Pop Rock

10

LET IT GO
from FROZEN

Music and Lyrics by
KRISTEN ANDERSON-LOPEZ and ROBERT LOPEZ

Half-Time Feel, Mysterious

© 2013 Wonderland Music Company, Inc.
All Rights Reserved.   Used by Permission.

WILDEST DREAMS

Words and Music by TAYLOR SWIFT,
MAX MARTIN and SHELLBACK

Moderately Fast

Copyright © 2014 SONGS OF UNIVERSAL, INC., TAYLOR SWIFT MUSIC, SONY MUSIC PUBLISHING (US) LLC, MXM and KMR MUSIC ROYALTIES II SCSP
This arrangement Copyright © 2023 SONGS OF UNIVERSAL, INC., TAYLOR SWIFT MUSIC, SONY MUSIC PUBLISHING (US) LLC, MXM and KMR MUSIC ROYALTIES II SCSP
All Rights for TAYLOR SWIFT MUSIC Administered by SONGS OF UNIVERSAL, INC.
All Rights for SONY MUSIC PUBLISHING (US) LLC Administered by SONY MUSIC PUBLISHING (US) LLC, 424 Church Street, Suite 1200, Nashville, TN 37219
All Rights for MXM and KMR MUSIC ROYALTIES II SCSP Administered Worldwide by Kobalt Songs Music Publishing
All Rights Reserved   Used by Permission.

I GOTTA FEELING

Words and Music by WILL ADAMS,
ALLAN PINEDA, JAIME GOMEZ, STACY FERGUSON,
DAVID GUETTA and FREDERIC RIESTERER

Moderately Fast

VIDA LA VIDA

Words and Music by
GUY BERRYMAN, JON BUCKLAND
WILL CHAMPION and CHRIS MARTIN

With Intensity

THIS IS ME
from THE GREATEST SHOWMAN

Words and Music by
BENJ PASEK and JUSTIN PAUL

With Emotion

WE ARE THE CHAMPIONS

Words and Music by
FREDDIE MERCURY

Moderately Slow

BLINDING LIGHTS

Words and Music by ABEL TESFAYE,
MAX MARTIN, JASON QUENNEVILLE,
OSCAR HOLTER and AHMAD BALSHE

Fast, Driving Retro Pop

DON'T STOP BELIEVIN'

Words and Music by STEVE PERRY,
NEAL SCHON and JONATHAN CAIN

Moderate Rock

NO TIME TO DIE
from NO TIME TO DIE

Words and Music by BILLIE EILISH O'CONNELL
and FINNEAS O'CONNELL

Moderately

LEAD THE WAY
from RAYA AND THE LAST DRAGON

Music and Lyrics by JHENE AIKO

Moderately

YOU WILL BE FOUND
from DEAR EVAN HANSEN

Music and Lyrics by
BENJ PASEK and JUSTIN PAUL

Reverent

THE IMPERIAL MARCH (Darth Vader's Theme)
from STAR WARS: THE EMPIRE STRIKES BACK

Music by JOHN WILLIAMS

March

BELIEVER

Words and Music by DAN REYNOLDS, WAYNE SERMON,
BEN MCKEE, DANIEL PLATZMAN, JUSTIN TRANTOR,
MATTIAS LARSSON and ROBIN FREDRICKSSON

Rock Shuffle!

ANGRY BIRDS THEME

By ARI PULKKINEN

Ooom-pah Style